AF255512

SUZANNE BYRD

Unlocking Potential: A Comprehensive Guide to Early Dyslexia Intervention

Empowering Parents, Educators, and Caregivers to Foster Literacy and Confidence in Young Learners

First edition

This book was professionally typeset on Reedsy.
Find out more at reedsy.com

Contents

1 Introduction   1

     Introduction: A Guide for Parents, Educators,
         and Caregivers   1

     Who Is This Book For?   1

     What Will This Book Achieve?   3

     The Benefits of Early Intervention   5

     What You Will Gain from This Book   5

2 Understanding Dyslexia in Early Childhood   7

     What is Dyslexia?   7

     Signs of Dyslexia in Preschoolers   9

     The Importance of Early Intervention   11

3 Building a Strong Foundation – Pre-Reading Skills   14

     Pre-Reading Skills: Building Blocks for Literacy   14

     Developing Phonological Awareness   15

     Alphabet Recognition   17

     Fostering a Love for Books   18

4 Introducing Phonics – Learning to Decode   21

     Phonics Instruction: A Key Tool for Dyslexic Learners   21

     What is Phonics?   21

     Why Phonics is Critical for Children with Dyslexia   22

     Strategies for Effective Phonics Instruction   23

     Multi-Sensory Phonics Instruction   24

     Blending Sounds to Read Words   26

     Segmenting Sounds to Spell Words   26

Objective: Help children practice segmenting
sounds in words.   27

5 Engaging Activities for Learning to Read   28
   Hands-On Activities to Support Reading Skills
       for Children with Dyslexia   28
   Rhyming Activities to Support Phonological Awareness   28
   Letter-Sound Matching Games   30
   Story Sequence Cards for Comprehension   31
   Sight Word Activities   32
   Additional Ideas for Hands-On Learning   33

6 Overcoming Challenges – Tips for Parents and Educators   35
   Encouraging Progress, Not Perfection   35
   Building Confidence Through Praise   36
   Creating a Dyslexia-Friendly Learning Environment   37
   Collaborating with Teachers and Specialists   38

7 Concluding Thoughts and Activities   39

8 Additional Resources   44
   Books to Read Aloud   44
   Apps and Tools for Pre-Readers   45
   Parent and Educator Support Networks   45
   Conclusion   46

1

Introduction

Introduction: A Guide for Parents, Educators, and Caregivers

Reading is one of the most essential skills children learn, opening doors to lifelong learning, creativity, and personal growth. However, for children with dyslexia, learning to read can be an especially challenging journey. This book, *"Teaching Young Minds: A Guide to Helping Children Aged 3-5 with Dyslexia Learn to Read – Engaging Activities Included,"* is designed specifically for parents, educators, and caregivers of children aged 3 to 5 who show signs of dyslexia or reading difficulties. It provides practical tools, strategies, and activities to support these children in developing strong pre-reading and reading skills from an early age.

Who Is This Book For?

This book is intended for anyone involved in the education or care of young children, particularly those who may have or are at risk of developing dyslexia. Whether you're a parent, preschool teacher, early intervention specialist, or caregiver, you play a critical role in supporting a child's early literacy development. The preschool years are a critical time for setting the foundation for future reading success, and by focusing on multi-sensory, engaging, and evidence-based strategies, this guide will help you give the children in your care the tools they need to succeed.

Parents

Parents of children with dyslexia often face a unique set of challenges. It can be heartbreaking to watch your child struggle with something as fundamental as reading, especially when traditional methods don't seem to work. This book provides clear, practical advice for parents who want to help their children thrive. By using the activities and strategies outlined in these chapters, you'll be able to support your child in developing early literacy skills in a fun and pressure-free way.

As a parent, you may feel unsure about how to approach teaching reading at home or how to recognize early signs of dyslexia in your child. This book will empower you with the knowledge to identify potential learning difficulties early on and the confidence to use simple, effective techniques that support your child's learning style. Additionally, you'll gain insight into how to collaborate with teachers, specialists, and other professionals to ensure that your child receives the best support both at home and in educational settings.

Educators and Caregivers

If you are a teacher or caregiver working with preschool-aged children, this book provides you with the tools you need to identify and address the early signs of dyslexia in your classroom or care environment. It's not always easy to recognize the subtle signs of dyslexia in children as young as three or four years old, but early intervention is crucial. This guide offers tips for creating a dyslexia-friendly learning environment and engaging all learners, regardless of their learning style.

The activities in this book are designed to be easily incorporated into the daily routines of preschoolers and young children, making them accessible even in busy classroom settings. Whether you are looking for phonics games, sensory activities, or story-time strategies, you'll find plenty of creative and research-backed methods to help children with dyslexia build confidence and enthusiasm for reading.

Specialists and Early Interventionists

Speech-language pathologists, reading specialists, and early interventionists can also benefit from the structured, multi-sensory activities in this book. These activities are designed to complement existing therapeutic or intervention approaches, offering additional ways to reinforce phonological awareness, phonics, and early literacy skills. By working closely with parents and teachers, specialists can help ensure that children receive consistent support across all areas of their lives.

What Will This Book Achieve?

The primary goal of this book is to give children with dyslexia the best possible start on their reading journey by focusing on early intervention during the critical years between ages 3 and 5. These years represent a vital window of opportunity to build the foundational skills children need for reading success. Children with dyslexia often require extra time and practice to develop these skills, and the sooner we begin supporting them, the more likely they are to experience positive outcomes as they transition into formal schooling.

Building Foundational Skills

This book will help you build key foundational literacy skills in young children. By focusing on phonological awareness (the ability to recognize and manipulate sounds in words), letter recognition, and the relationship between letters and sounds (phonics), you can help lay the groundwork for successful reading development. Children with dyslexia often struggle in these areas, and by using the techniques in this book, you'll provide them with the support they need to overcome early challenges.

Making Learning Fun

Children learn best when they are engaged, and this book emphasizes making reading instruction fun and interactive. The activities in each chapter are designed to be multi-sensory, meaning they engage multiple senses—sight, sound, touch, and movement. This type of learning is especially beneficial for children with dyslexia, who often find it difficult to retain information presented through only one sensory channel.

By using activities like rhyming games, sensory letter tracing, and story sequencing, you'll make reading feel less like a chore and more like a playful adventure. When children enjoy the learning process, they are more motivated to persist through challenges and are more likely to develop a positive attitude toward reading.

Supporting Confidence and Reducing Frustration

Children with dyslexia often face frustration when they struggle to keep up with peers in traditional learning environments. This book aims to reduce that frustration by offering targeted strategies that are tailored to their specific learning needs. Through repetition, practice, and encouragement, you'll help build the child's confidence in their ability to read, even if they encounter difficulties along the way.

By focusing on progress rather than perfection, this book encourages a growth mindset—children learn that effort and persistence lead to improvement, which can boost their self-esteem and foster a sense of pride in their accomplishments.

The Benefits of Early Intervention

Research consistently shows that early intervention is one of the most effective ways to help children with dyslexia succeed. When children receive support in developing reading skills at an early age, they are less likely to experience the academic and emotional difficulties that can arise from struggling with reading later in life. Early intervention can prevent the "wait-to-fail" approach, where children fall behind their peers before receiving help. By starting early, we can ensure that children with dyslexia have the tools they need before formal reading instruction begins in school.

This book focuses on providing strategies and activities that can be implemented before a child enters kindergarten or first grade, when formal reading instruction typically begins. By working on pre-reading skills, such as phonological awareness and letter-sound recognition, you'll give children the best chance to develop the necessary skills to read fluently and confidently.

What You Will Gain from This Book

By the time you finish reading this book, you will:

- **Understand dyslexia in early childhood**: You'll learn about the early signs of dyslexia, why it happens, and how it affects reading development.

- **Feel confident in supporting early readers**: Whether you're a parent, teacher, or specialist, you'll gain practical strategies for helping children build foundational literacy skills, tailored to their unique needs.

- **Be equipped with engaging activities**: You'll have access to a wide range of fun, multi-sensory activities designed to reinforce reading skills in a playful and low-pressure way.

- **Know how to create a supportive environment**: You'll learn how to create a dyslexia-friendly learning environment that fosters confidence, minimizes frustration, and encourages a love of books and stories.

- **Develop a partnership with specialists**: You'll understand how to collaborate with reading specialists, speech therapists, and educators to create a consistent support system for children with dyslexia.

2

Understanding Dyslexia in Early Childhood

What is Dyslexia?

Dyslexia is one of the most common specific learning disabilities, affecting the ability to read, write, and spell. It has a neurobiological basis, meaning it stems from differences in the way the brain processes language. Dyslexia is not tied to intelligence. In fact, many individuals with dyslexia demonstrate remarkable strengths in areas such as problem-solving, creativity, and visual-spatial thinking. Despite these strengths, they face persistent challenges with phonological processing—the ability to break down words into individual sounds (phonemes) and associate these sounds with letters or letter patterns. This difficulty forms the core of their struggle with reading.

Understanding Phonological Processing

Phonological processing refers to the brain's ability to break words into their constituent sounds and match those sounds to written symbols. For example, in the word "cat," phonological processing allows a child to identify the sounds /k/, /a/, and /t/, and then match them with the letters "C," "A," and "T." In children with dyslexia, this process does not happen as efficiently or accurately. They may have trouble distinguishing between similar sounds, such as the difference between /b/ and /p/, or they might struggle to blend sounds together to form whole words. This results in slower, more effortful reading and makes it difficult for children with dyslexia to develop automatic word recognition skills.

Common Misunderstandings About Dyslexia

Dyslexia is often misunderstood, leading to misconceptions that can affect how children with the condition are perceived and supported. One of the most prevalent myths is that dyslexia causes people to see letters or words backward. While it is true that some children with dyslexia may reverse letters or confuse similarly shaped letters (such as "b" and "d"), this is not a defining characteristic of dyslexia and is something that typically resolves with practice. Dyslexia is not a visual problem but a language-based one. It involves challenges in recognizing sounds, blending sounds into words, and retrieving the correct words from memory.

Dyslexic children may struggle with tasks like rhyming or breaking words down into sounds, which can make learning the alphabet and basic phonics difficult. However, it's important to recognize that dyslexia affects each child differently. Some may have mild difficulties, while others may face more significant challenges that require intensive support.

Neuroscientific Insights into Dyslexia

Advances in neuroscience have provided valuable insights into the brain differences that underlie dyslexia. Brain imaging studies show that when children with dyslexia engage in reading tasks, they activate different areas of the brain than children without dyslexia. Typically, proficient readers use the brain's left hemisphere, which contains regions specialized for processing language and phonology. In contrast, children with dyslexia often recruit areas of the brain in the right hemisphere or different parts of the left hemisphere that are not as efficient for reading tasks.

This difference in brain activation may explain why reading feels more effortful and time-consuming for children with dyslexia. Instead of using the brain's more streamlined language-processing pathways, they are compensating by using other areas of the brain, which makes reading slower and more laborious. The good news is that with the right interventions, the brain can be trained to develop new pathways for reading. This is why early intervention is so important—it helps to rewire the brain for more efficient reading.

Signs of Dyslexia in Preschoolers

Dyslexia is a lifelong condition, but its signs can appear as early as preschool. Recognizing these early signs is crucial because early intervention can significantly improve a child's reading outcomes. Children between the ages of 3 and 5 who show signs of dyslexia may struggle with language-related tasks long before formal reading instruction begins. Although a definitive diagnosis is not usually made until later, observing certain behaviors in preschool-aged children can help identify those who may benefit from early support.

Delayed Speech Development

One of the earliest signs of dyslexia can be delayed speech development. Many children with dyslexia are late talkers compared to their peers. They may struggle to learn to speak, have difficulty pronouncing words, or exhibit problems with word retrieval, such as substituting words or pausing frequently while talking. This delay is often related to the phonological processing issues that underlie dyslexia. Because they have trouble breaking down and manipulating sounds, they may also struggle to produce and use language effectively.

Difficulty Learning Letters and Sounds

Another hallmark sign of dyslexia in preschoolers is difficulty with letter and sound recognition. Even after repeated exposure to the alphabet, children with dyslexia may have trouble remembering the names of letters or associating letters with their corresponding sounds. For example, a child might struggle to recognize that the letter "B" makes the /b/ sound or might confuse similar-sounding letters like "B" and "P." This difficulty is directly tied to the phonological deficits that are central to dyslexia, making it harder for these children to grasp the basic building blocks of reading.

Trouble with Rhyming

Phonological awareness—the ability to recognize and manipulate sounds in words—is often impaired in children with dyslexia. One of the earliest indicators of this is trouble with rhyming. While most preschoolers enjoy playing with rhymes and can easily recognize that "cat" and "bat" sound alike, children with dyslexia may struggle to hear or produce rhyming words. This is because they have difficulty isolating and identifying the individual sounds within words, which is necessary for recognizing sound patterns like rhymes.

Poor Memory for Sequencing

Children with dyslexia may also exhibit poor memory for sequencing tasks. For instance, they might have trouble remembering the days of the week in order, recounting the steps in a familiar routine, or telling a story in the correct sequence of events. This difficulty can also extend to remembering the sequence of sounds in a word, which is why they may mispronounce words or struggle to blend sounds together when reading.

Difficulty Learning New Vocabulary

Learning and retaining new vocabulary can be a challenge for children with dyslexia. Words that are long, complex, or phonetically irregular may be particularly difficult to learn. Even after being exposed to a new word multiple times, a child with dyslexia may have trouble recalling it or pronouncing it correctly. This difficulty with vocabulary acquisition is linked to the underlying phonological and memory deficits associated with dyslexia.

While it's too early to diagnose dyslexia definitively in preschool-aged children, these early signs can signal the need for additional support. By addressing these difficulties early on with a multi-sensory, language-rich approach, caregivers can give children a strong foundation for future literacy development.

The Importance of Early Intervention

Early intervention is critical for children with dyslexia. The brain is incredibly plastic in early childhood, meaning that with the right support, it can form new pathways to process language more efficiently. Early intervention can prevent the frustration and discouragement that often accompany reading struggles later on. It also gives children the tools and strategies they need to build confidence in their reading abilities.

Research consistently shows that children who receive targeted support before formal reading instruction begins tend to make faster progress in reading than those who don't receive help until later. Early literacy experiences, such as being read to, engaging in language-rich conversations, and playing with sounds, are essential for building the foundational skills necessary for reading success.

Strategies for Early Intervention

1. **Multi-Sensory Learning**: Multi-sensory instruction is a highly effective approach for children with dyslexia. By using all of their senses—sight, sound, touch, and even movement—children can reinforce their understanding of letters, sounds, and words. For example, children might learn the letter "A" by seeing it, hearing its sound, tracing it in the air, and building it with playdough. This approach helps to strengthen the connections between sounds and symbols, making it easier for children with dyslexia to process language.

2. **Repetition and Consistency**: Children with dyslexia often need more repetition to learn and retain new information. Incorporating daily practice with letters, sounds, and words in a fun and engaging way helps solidify these skills. Consistency is key, as repeated exposure to concepts over time helps children form lasting connections.

3. **Speech-Language Therapy**: For some children, working with a speech-language therapist can be beneficial, especially if they are experiencing difficulties with phonological awareness or vocabulary development. Speech therapists use targeted techniques to

help children improve their ability to break down sounds in words, recall vocabulary, and strengthen their overall language skills.

By understanding what dyslexia is and recognizing its early signs, caregivers, educators, and specialists can intervene early and give children the support they need to succeed in reading.

3

Building a Strong Foundation – Pre-Reading Skills

Pre-Reading Skills: Building Blocks for Literacy

Pre-reading skills are essential building blocks that set the stage for future reading success. These foundational skills include phonological awareness, alphabet recognition, and cultivating a positive relationship with books. For children with dyslexia, developing these pre-reading skills is especially critical, as these areas often present significant challenges. By focusing on strengthening these skills in early childhood, we can provide children with the tools they need to become confident readers. This chapter will explore the core components of pre-reading skills and provide practical strategies and activities to support children, particularly those with dyslexia, in their early literacy journey.

Developing Phonological Awareness

Phonological awareness is one of the most important predictors of later reading success. It refers to a child's ability to recognize and manipulate the sounds within spoken words. These skills include the ability to recognize rhymes, identify the first and last sounds in words, and break words down into individual phonemes (the smallest units of sound). Phonological awareness is a precursor to phonics, the understanding that sounds in words correspond to letters.

For children with dyslexia, phonological awareness often presents the most significant challenge. Phonemic awareness, a subset of phonological awareness, is the ability to hear, identify, and manipulate individual phonemes in words. This is crucial for learning to decode words when reading. A child with strong phonemic awareness understands, for example, that the word "cat" is made up of three distinct sounds: /k/, /a/, and /t/. However, children with dyslexia often struggle with phonemic awareness, which makes decoding and reading difficult.

Strategies for Developing Phonological Awareness

Developing phonological awareness is a key focus for young children, especially those with dyslexia. Below are strategies and activities that can be used to build these critical skills in a fun and engaging way.

- **Sound Sorting**: This activity helps children become aware of the different sounds at the beginning of words. You can create simple sound-sorting activities where children group objects or pictures based on their initial sounds. For example, you might gather pictures of a cat, cow, and cup, and ask the child to identify that they all start with the /k/ sound. This task encourages children to pay attention to how words begin and helps build their ability to distinguish individual sounds.

- **Clapping Syllables**: Another effective way to develop phonological awareness is through syllable segmentation. By clapping out the syllables in words, children begin to understand that words are made up of smaller parts. For instance, when you say the word "butterfly," the child would clap three times for the three syllables: "but-ter-fly." This activity is easy to incorporate into daily routines and helps children learn to break down words into manageable chunks.

- **Rhyming Games**: Rhyming games can also boost phonological awareness. These games encourage children to listen for patterns in sound. A simple rhyming game might involve asking a child to think of words that rhyme with a target word. For example, you might say, "What rhymes with 'cat'? Bat, hat, mat!" Rhyming helps children become more attuned to the similarities in word sounds, a skill that will support later phonics learning.

Activity: Sound Detective

This fun and interactive game helps children focus on the beginning and ending sounds of words.

- **Objective**: Develop the ability to identify beginning and ending sounds in words.
- **Materials**: Picture cards with images such as a cat, dog, and bus.
- **Instructions**: Show the child a picture card, say the word aloud, and ask, "What sound does this word start with?" For example, when showing a picture of a cat, emphasize the initial /k/ sound. Once the child can identify the first sound, move on to identifying the ending sound. Slowly say the word "cat" and ask the child to listen for the last sound (/t/). You can also make this a guessing

game by offering clues, such as, "I spy something that starts with /k/" (while showing the picture of a cat). This game strengthens auditory discrimination and helps children connect sounds with words.

Alphabet Recognition

Alphabet recognition refers to the ability to recognize letters by their names and associate them with the sounds they represent. This skill is fundamental to reading and writing. Children with dyslexia often struggle to learn the alphabet because they find it difficult to link letter symbols with their corresponding sounds. A multi-sensory approach—where children engage their sight, sound, touch, and even movement—can make learning the alphabet more accessible and enjoyable for these children.

Strategies for Building Alphabet Recognition

Alphabet recognition can be developed through a variety of playful and tactile activities. Here are some strategies that focus on engaging multiple senses to reinforce learning:

- **Letter of the Week**: Focusing on one letter each week allows children to fully immerse themselves in learning that letter. You can introduce the letter in different contexts throughout the week, such as finding it in books, tracing it in sand, and even incorporating it into art projects or songs. By immersing the child in multiple experiences with the letter, they begin to form stronger connections between the letter's name, shape, and sound.
- **Tactile Letters**: Using textured letters made from materials such as sandpaper or fabric gives children a tactile experience of letter

learning. Encourage the child to trace the letter with their finger while saying the sound aloud. This tactile experience helps reinforce both the visual shape of the letter and its sound, making it easier for the child to retain the information.

Activity: Sensory Letter Tracing

This activity is an excellent way to improve letter recognition and sound association through a tactile, multi-sensory approach.

- **Objective**: Enhance letter recognition and sound association using a tactile method.
- **Materials**: Sandpaper letters and a tray of sand or rice.
- **Instructions**: Have the child trace the letter on sandpaper while saying the sound aloud. Then, invite them to trace the same letter in the sand or rice. This activity combines visual, tactile, and auditory learning, which helps children with dyslexia strengthen their letter recognition and phonics skills. By engaging multiple senses, children are more likely to retain the information and apply it when they encounter letters in other contexts.

Fostering a Love for Books

For children with dyslexia, learning to read can be a frustrating experience. That's why it's important to foster a love for books and stories from an early age. Reading aloud to children and providing positive experiences with books not only helps them develop a love for language but also exposes them to rich vocabulary, new ideas, and the joy of storytelling. Building a positive relationship with books is crucial because it helps counterbalance the frustration children with dyslexia might feel when they begin formal reading instruction.

Strategies for Fostering a Love of Books

Encouraging a love for reading starts with creating enjoyable, interactive experiences with books. Below are some strategies that make reading an engaging and pleasant activity:

- **Interactive Read-Alouds**: Choose books with repetitive phrases or rhymes that encourage participation. For instance, in a book like *"Brown Bear, Brown Bear, What Do You See?"*, pause and let the child fill in the repeated phrase. These interactive moments make reading feel like a shared activity rather than a one-way experience, and they help children become more engaged in the story.
- **Picture Walks**: Before reading a new book, take the child on a "picture walk" through the pages. This involves looking at the pictures together and discussing what might happen in the story, without focusing on the text just yet. This strategy helps the child engage with the book in a low-pressure way and encourages them to think critically about the story before encountering any challenging words.

Further Activities

This activity turns reading into an exciting adventure by encouraging children to connect the story with real-life objects.

- **Objective**: Build engagement with books and reinforce vocabulary.
- **Materials**: A favorite picture book and everyday objects.
- **Instructions**: Choose a book that mentions objects commonly found around the house or classroom. As you read the story aloud, invite the child to find those objects in the room. For example, if the story mentions a red ball, encourage the child to search for a

red ball in their environment. This interactive experience helps the child connect the words and concepts in the story with real-life objects, making reading more engaging and meaningful.

4

Introducing Phonics – Learning to Decode

Phonics Instruction: A Key Tool for Dyslexic Learners

Phonics instruction teaches children the relationship between letters and sounds, providing them with the tools they need to decode unfamiliar words by sounding them out. This skill is particularly important for children with dyslexia, who often struggle with recognizing words by sight alone. For these learners, a systematic and explicit approach to phonics is essential, as they benefit from clear, step-by-step instruction in the sound-letter correspondence that underpins reading and writing. By focusing on phonics, we can give children with dyslexia the building blocks they need to become confident, independent readers.

What is Phonics?

Phonics is a method of teaching reading that emphasizes the relationship between the letters of the alphabet and their corresponding sounds. It involves teaching children to recognize individual sounds, or phonemes, and the letters or letter combinations, known as graphemes, that represent these sounds. Phonics instruction enables children to break down words into their component sounds, allowing them to decode unfamiliar words by blending these sounds together.

For example, the word "cat" can be broken down into three phonemes: /k/, /a/, and /t/. Phonics instruction teaches children how to match each sound with its corresponding letter, helping them understand how to read words they have not encountered before. This decoding ability is particularly important for children with dyslexia, who often struggle with memorizing words by sight. Instead of relying on memory, phonics gives these children a strategy for figuring out unfamiliar words.

Why Phonics is Critical for Children with Dyslexia

Children with dyslexia typically have difficulty with phonemic awareness, which is the foundation of phonics. Phonemic awareness refers to the ability to hear, identify, and manipulate individual sounds in words. Without strong phonemic awareness, children may struggle to understand how the sounds in words relate to the letters they see on the page. This difficulty can make it hard for them to recognize patterns in language and read fluently.

When children with dyslexia lack strong phonics skills, they are more likely to guess words based on context or visual cues, which can lead to frustration and errors. Guessing strategies do not provide long-term solutions, as they do not equip children with the tools they need to independently decode new words. By contrast, explicit and systematic phonics instruction gives these children a reliable method for breaking down words and sounding them out, which improves both their reading accuracy and confidence.

Strategies for Effective Phonics Instruction

A systematic and structured approach is critical for phonics instruction, especially for children with dyslexia. Below are some strategies that can help ensure phonics instruction is effective for dyslexic learners:

Structured Literacy Approach

The structured literacy approach is particularly effective for dyslexic learners because it involves teaching phonics in a systematic and explicit manner. This method starts with the simplest sounds and gradually progresses to more complex letter-sound combinations. By breaking phonics instruction into manageable steps, children are able to build a strong foundation of knowledge that they can draw upon as they encounter more challenging words.

In structured literacy, each phonics concept is taught explicitly, ensuring that children understand each sound-letter relationship before moving on to the next. For example, instruction might begin with simple consonant-vowel-consonant (CVC) words like "cat" or "dog," before introducing more complex patterns such as consonant blends (e.g., "bl" or "tr") and vowel teams (e.g., "ea" in "team"). This structured, scaffolded approach gives children the time and practice they need to master each concept.

Multi-Sensory Techniques

Multi-sensory learning techniques are particularly effective for children with dyslexia because they engage multiple senses—sight, sound, touch, and sometimes even movement—to reinforce phonics concepts. These techniques allow children to process information through different channels, making it easier for them to retain and apply what they have learned.

For example, a child learning the letter "S" might first see the letter (visual), then hear the sound it makes (/s/) (auditory), and finally trace the letter with their finger (tactile). This multi-sensory approach helps children form stronger connections between letters and sounds, improving both their ability to recognize letters and their overall phonics skills.

Repetition and Practice

Children with dyslexia often need more repetition and practice than their peers to solidify their understanding of phonics rules. This can be done through games, flashcards, and reading practice with decodable texts—texts specifically designed to align with the phonics patterns the child is learning. Repetition allows children to practice applying the phonics skills they've learned in various contexts, reinforcing their understanding and helping them become more confident readers.

For instance, after learning a new sound-letter correspondence, children can practice reading words that include that letter-sound pattern. Decodable texts are particularly useful for this purpose, as they contain words that are closely matched to the child's current phonics knowledge, giving them the opportunity to apply what they've learned in a controlled setting.

Multi-Sensory Phonics Instruction

As mentioned, multi-sensory instruction is especially effective for children with dyslexia because it taps into multiple areas of the brain. This helps children retain and apply what they've learned, improving their ability to decode words. By combining visual, auditory, and tactile experiences, multi-sensory instruction engages children in active learning, making it easier for them to grasp phonics concepts.

For example, a child might learn the sound-letter relationship for the letter "S" by first seeing the letter written on a card, then listening to the teacher pronounce the /s/ sound, and finally tracing the letter with their finger while saying the sound aloud. Engaging in these activities simultaneously helps reinforce the connection between the letter and its sound, making it more likely that the child will remember and apply this knowledge when reading.

Practical Activity: Letter-Sound Treasure Hunt

One fun way to reinforce letter-sound correspondence is through a treasure hunt activity.

- Objective: Reinforce letter-sound correspondence in a fun, engaging way.
- Materials: Cards with letters and pictures of objects that start with each letter (e.g., A for apple, B for ball).

Instructions: Hide the letter cards around a room or outdoor space. Ask the child to find a letter card and match it with a picture of an object that starts with the same sound. For example, the child might find the letter "C" and match it with a picture of a cat. This activity engages children in a hands-on learning experience that reinforces their ability to recognize letters and their sounds.

Blending Sounds to Read Words

Blending is the process of combining individual sounds to form whole words. Once children with dyslexia have learned individual letter sounds, the next step is to teach them how to blend these sounds together. Blending is a key skill in phonics instruction, as it allows children to move from sounding out letters in isolation to reading smoothly and fluently.

Practical Activity: Sound Blending Train

The Sound Blending Train activity helps children practice blending sounds to form words.

- Objective: Help children practice blending sounds to form words.
- Materials: Letter cards or magnetic letters.
- Instructions: Line up several letter cards to form a simple word (e.g., "cat").

Say each sound separately (/k/ /a/ /t/), then blend the sounds together to form the word "cat." Encourage the child to move their finger along the letters as they blend the sounds together. This activity helps children practice the essential skill of blending sounds to read words.

Segmenting Sounds to Spell Words

In addition to blending sounds to read, children with dyslexia also need practice segmenting sounds to spell words. Segmenting involves breaking words down into their individual sounds, which helps children understand the relationship between spoken words and their written forms.

Practical Activity: Word Stretching

Word Stretching is a helpful activity for teaching children how to segment words into individual sounds.

Objective: Help children practice segmenting sounds in words.

Materials: Counters or small objects, letter cards.

Instructions: Say a simple word (e.g., "dog") and ask the child to stretch out the sounds (/d/ /o/ /g/). For each sound they hear, they place a counter or object in front of them. Then, have the child match the sounds with letters by placing the corresponding letter cards in front of the objects. This activity helps children understand how words are made up of individual sounds and how those sounds correspond to letters.

Phonics instruction is a powerful tool for helping children with dyslexia develop strong reading skills. By using a systematic, multi-sensory approach that emphasizes repetition and practice, children can learn to decode words and build the confidence they need to become successful readers. Whether through blending sounds to read or segmenting sounds to spell, phonics gives children with dyslexia the foundation they need to succeed in literacy.

5

Engaging Activities for Learning to Read

Hands-On Activities to Support Reading Skills for Children with Dyslexia

Children with dyslexia often benefit most from engaging, interactive, and hands-on learning experiences. Since dyslexia affects how the brain processes language, activities that incorporate movement, creativity, and multi-sensory engagement can help reinforce reading concepts in a way that feels natural and enjoyable for the child. This chapter focuses on activities designed to make learning fun, accessible, and effective for young children, particularly those with dyslexia. By incorporating these strategies, children can practice and strengthen their reading skills in a low-pressure, engaging environment.

Rhyming Activities to Support Phonological Awareness

Phonological awareness is a crucial pre-reading skill, and one way to develop it is through rhyming activities. Rhyming helps children understand how sounds work together in words. For children with dyslexia, rhyming can be challenging because they often struggle with hearing and manipulating sounds within words. Engaging children in fun rhyming activities helps build this foundational skill, making it easier for them to grasp the concept of how sounds form words.

Why Rhyming is Important

Rhyming is more than just wordplay; it helps children understand sound patterns, which are essential for learning how to decode and read words. When children can recognize that "cat," "hat," and "bat" share the same ending sounds, they begin to form the foundation for phonics skills, where letter patterns correspond to sound patterns.

Practical Activity: Rhyming Word Hopscotch

- **Objective**: Improve phonological awareness and rhyming skills.
- **Materials**: Outdoor chalk or masking tape, words written on cards or boards.
- **Instructions**: Draw a hopscotch grid on the ground, writing simple rhyming words (e.g., "cat," "bat," "hat") in each square. Call out one of the words, and ask the child to hop to a square with a word that rhymes. As they hop, have them say the rhyming words aloud. For example, if you call out "cat," the child might hop to "bat" and say both words aloud. This activity combines physical movement with language learning, making it an enjoyable way to reinforce rhyming skills. The active, playful nature of the game helps children with dyslexia stay engaged while reinforcing their understanding of rhyming patterns.

Letter-Sound Matching Games

One of the most fundamental reading skills is learning how to match letters with the sounds they represent. This skill forms the basis of phonics and is crucial for early readers, particularly for children with dyslexia, who often struggle with this connection. Incorporating letter-sound matching into games turns practice into play, making it more enjoyable for children while reducing frustration.

Why Letter-Sound Correspondence is Important

For children with dyslexia, learning to associate letters with their corresponding sounds can be challenging. They may confuse similar-looking letters (e.g., "b" and "d") or struggle to remember the sound each letter represents. Mastering letter-sound correspondence is essential for reading fluency because it allows children to decode unfamiliar words more easily.

Practical Activity: Sound Matching Puzzles

Objective: Strengthen letter-sound correspondence.

Materials: Picture puzzle pieces with an image on one side and the first letter of the word on the other side.

Instructions: Create or purchase a set of puzzle pieces with pictures on one side and the corresponding first letter of the word on the other. For example, a picture of a dog would have a puzzle piece with the letter "D." The goal is for the child to match the picture piece with the letter that corresponds to the initial sound of the word. This activity helps children practice associating sounds with letters, reinforcing the concept that each letter represents a sound in words. By matching the pictures and letters, children with dyslexia engage in a multi-sensory experience that strengthens their understanding of letter-sound correspondence.

Story Sequence Cards for Comprehension

Reading comprehension is often an area of difficulty for children with dyslexia. While their focus may be on decoding individual words, they can miss the broader meaning of a text. Story sequencing activities help children understand the structure and flow of a story, building their comprehension skills by encouraging them to think about events in order and how they connect to one another.

Why Story Sequencing is Important

For children with dyslexia, the effort involved in decoding each word can detract from understanding the overall meaning of a story. Sequencing activities help shift their focus toward the narrative, encouraging them to see stories as a cohesive whole rather than isolated words. By focusing on the structure of a story, children strengthen their ability to understand and remember what they've read.

Practical Activity: Story Sequence Cards

- **Objective**: Build comprehension and sequencing skills.
- **Materials**: A set of cards with pictures representing key events in a story.
- **Instructions**: After reading a short story aloud, give the child a set of cards that depict the major events of the story, but in a mixed-up order. Ask the child to arrange the cards in the correct sequence based on the story they just heard. Once they've arranged

the cards, discuss the order of events and ask questions to reinforce comprehension. For example, ask, "What happened first?" or "Why did the character do that?" This activity encourages children to think about the structure of stories and helps strengthen their understanding of narrative flow, a key component of reading comprehension.

Sight Word Activities

Sight words are words that often don't follow standard phonics rules and must be memorized because they are frequently used in text (e.g., "the," "said," "come"). Many children with dyslexia struggle to recognize sight words, which can hinder reading fluency. Making sight word practice fun through games can help children memorize these words more easily.

Why Sight Words Matter

Because sight words appear frequently in early reading materials, recognizing them instantly is important for fluency. Children who cannot recognize sight words quickly often lose momentum when reading, which can lead to frustration. By making sight word recognition automatic, children can focus more on comprehension rather than getting stuck on common, irregularly spelled words.

Practical Activity: Sight Word Bingo

- **Objective**: Improve sight word recognition.
- **Materials**: Bingo cards with sight words, markers or tokens.
- **Instructions**: Create bingo cards using common sight words

instead of numbers. As you call out each sight word, the child places a marker on the matching word on their bingo card. To keep the game interactive, you can vary how you call out the words—use them in a sentence, give a clue about the word's meaning, or simply say the word aloud. This activity helps reinforce sight word recognition in a fun and interactive way. The repetitive nature of the game helps children with dyslexia memorize and retain the words more effectively, building their sight word vocabulary over time.

Additional Ideas for Hands-On Learning

In addition to the activities listed above, there are many other ways to incorporate hands-on learning into reading practice for children with dyslexia. Below are a few more ideas:

- **Word Building with Manipulatives**: Use magnetic letters, letter tiles, or even letter blocks to help children build words. This tactile activity helps reinforce the connection between letters and sounds while allowing children to manipulate the letters physically, which can be particularly beneficial for dyslexic learners.
- **Interactive Storytelling**: After reading a book, have children act out scenes or use puppets to retell the story. This reinforces comprehension and helps them engage with the narrative on a deeper level.
- **Word Scavenger Hunt**: Create a scavenger hunt where children search for specific sight words or words that contain a certain letter-sound pattern around the room or house. This physical activity keeps children moving while reinforcing their reading skills.

For children with dyslexia, hands-on, interactive activities can make all the difference when it comes to developing reading skills. By turning reading practice into engaging games and experiences, you can help these children strengthen their phonological awareness, letter-sound correspondence, comprehension, and sight word recognition. The key is to make learning enjoyable and accessible, giving children with dyslexia the confidence and tools they need to succeed as readers. Through consistent, playful practice, these activities can provide children with the solid foundation they need to thrive in their literacy journey.

6

Overcoming Challenges – Tips for Parents and Educators

Supporting a child with dyslexia requires patience, encouragement, and adaptability. In this chapter, we will discuss practical strategies for overcoming the common challenges children with dyslexia face when learning to read.

Encouraging Progress, Not Perfection

Children with dyslexia often feel frustrated when they struggle to read, especially if they compare themselves to peers who are progressing faster. It's important to create a supportive environment where effort is praised, and small victories are celebrated.

Strategies for Encouraging Progress:

- **Focus on Effort Over Results**: Instead of focusing solely on whether the child got a word right or wrong, praise their effort. For example, say, "I love how hard you worked to sound out that word!" This reinforces the idea that learning to read is a process, and effort

35

is key to success.

- **Set Small, Achievable Goals**: Break reading tasks into small, manageable steps. Celebrate when the child reaches each milestone, whether it's learning a new sight word or decoding a tricky word. Small successes build confidence over time.

Building Confidence Through Praise

Children with dyslexia need to feel successful and confident to maintain their motivation to read. Praise plays a powerful role in building this confidence, but it's important to be specific in your praise.

Tips for Giving Effective Praise:

- **Be Specific**: Instead of saying, "Good job,"

say something more specific, such as, "I'm so proud of how you sounded out each letter in that word," or "I love how you didn't give up when the word was hard." Specific praise helps the child understand exactly what they did well and reinforces positive behaviors and strategies.

- **Praise Effort and Perseverance**: It's important to focus on the child's hard work and determination, rather than just the outcome. For example, if a child is struggling with a word but keeps trying, you can say, "You are working so hard to figure that out. Keep going, and you'll get it!" This builds a growth mindset, where children understand that their efforts will lead to improvement over time.
- **Balance Praise with Gentle Correction**: While praise is important, it's also necessary to guide the child when they make mistakes. However, this should be done in a supportive way that doesn't discourage them. For example, if a child misreads a word, you

could say, "That's close! Let's try sounding it out together one more time." This keeps the child motivated to keep trying without feeling discouraged.

Creating a Dyslexia-Friendly Learning Environment

A dyslexia-friendly learning environment is one that minimizes distractions, supports the child's unique learning needs, and provides opportunities for success. It's important to remember that children with dyslexia may take longer to complete reading tasks and may need additional support, so creating a calm, supportive, and structured learning space is essential.

Strategies for Creating a Dyslexia-Friendly Environment:

- **Minimize Distractions**: Children with dyslexia often benefit from a quiet, distraction-free environment when working on reading tasks. Make sure the child's workspace is free from noise, visual clutter, or interruptions that could make it harder for them to focus.
- **Use Visual Aids**: Many children with dyslexia are strong visual learners. Incorporating visual aids, such as picture books, charts, and posters with phonics rules, can help reinforce learning. Color-coded materials (e.g., using different colors for vowels and consonants) can also make it easier for children to recognize patterns in words.
- **Provide Extra Time**: Dyslexic children often need more time to process written language, so it's important to allow for extra time on reading and writing tasks. This reduces pressure and allows the child to work at their own pace.
- **Offer Multi-Sensory Materials**: Incorporating multi-sensory learning materials, such as textured letters, sand trays, or apps that

combine visuals with audio, can help children with dyslexia engage with reading in a way that makes sense to their learning style.

Collaborating with Teachers and Specialists

It's important for parents and educators to work together in supporting children with dyslexia. If a child is in preschool or early elementary school, collaborating with teachers, reading specialists, and other professionals can ensure the child receives consistent support in all learning environments.

Strategies for Collaboration:

- **Regular Communication**: Parents and teachers should maintain regular communication to discuss the child's progress and any challenges they are facing. Teachers can provide insights into how the child is performing in class, while parents can share what is working well at home.
- **Reading Specialists and Speech Therapists**: In some cases, children with dyslexia may benefit from working with reading specialists or speech-language pathologists. These professionals can provide targeted instruction in areas such as phonics, fluency, and phonological awareness. If a child is receiving extra support, it's important for parents and teachers to coordinate with these specialists to ensure a consistent approach to learning.
- **Encouraging Self-Advocacy**: As children with dyslexia grow older, they can be taught to advocate for their own learning needs. Encourage children to express when they need help, ask questions, or request additional time. Teaching self-advocacy early helps children build confidence in managing their dyslexia and navigating the school environment.

7

Concluding Thoughts and Activities

Teaching a child to read is one of the most meaningful and impactful journeys you can undertake. For children with dyslexia, this journey may come with unique challenges, but it also offers opportunities for growth, creativity, and resilience. As a parent, educator, or caregiver of a child with dyslexia, your role in shaping this journey is vital. The strategies, activities, and insights offered in this book have been designed to empower you with the tools you need to guide young learners through their early literacy development, fostering confidence and joy along the way.

The Power of Early Intervention

One of the most important takeaways from this book is the critical role of early intervention. Children with dyslexia often experience frustration and anxiety around reading if they aren't provided with the appropriate support early on. By recognizing the signs of dyslexia in the preschool years and addressing these challenges head-on, you can help a child avoid the pitfalls of falling behind, feeling discouraged, or believing that they're not capable of learning to read.

Early intervention does not just focus on academic achievement; it also plays a significant role in shaping a child's emotional relationship with learning. When we provide children with the right tools and strategies early on, we show them that reading is something they *can* do—it may take more effort, but it is achievable. This helps to build resilience and fosters a growth mindset, where children understand that challenges are not permanent obstacles, but opportunities to learn and grow.

Building Confidence Through Multi-Sensory Learning

Throughout this book, we've emphasized the importance of using multi-sensory learning techniques. For children with dyslexia, engaging multiple senses—sight, sound, touch, and movement—makes abstract concepts like letters, sounds, and words more concrete and easier to understand. These approaches also make learning more interactive and enjoyable, helping to alleviate the frustration that many children with dyslexia experience during reading instruction.

Whether you're using activities like sensory letter tracing, rhyming word hopscotch, or story sequencing cards, the aim is to provide children with a variety of ways to engage with language. When learning is fun and varied, children are more likely to stay motivated and curious. By tapping into different sensory modalities, you are helping children make lasting connections that strengthen their understanding of phonics, phonological awareness, and other essential literacy skills.

The multi-sensory approach also ensures that children with dyslexia are not left feeling like their learning differences are a barrier to success. Instead, they come to understand that there are multiple ways to approach reading, and that their unique learning style is just one of many valid paths to literacy. This mindset shift is crucial not only for their academic success but also for their self-esteem and overall confidence.

Creating a Supportive Learning Environment

A dyslexia-friendly learning environment is one that fosters patience, encouragement, and positivity. As we've discussed in previous chapters, children with dyslexia need a space where they feel safe to make mistakes, take their time, and learn at their own pace. It's important to remember that progress may be slower for children with dyslexia, but it is still progress, and every small step forward should be celebrated.

In a supportive learning environment, the emphasis is not on perfection, but on effort and perseverance. Children who are praised for their hard work, determination, and willingness to keep trying are more likely to develop a growth mindset. This mindset, which values effort over innate ability, helps children understand that success is within their reach if they continue to practice and learn.

Your role as a parent, teacher, or caregiver is to be a steady source of support and encouragement. When a child feels that the adults in their life believe in their abilities, they are more likely to believe in themselves. By offering gentle guidance, specific praise, and ample opportunities for practice, you create a learning environment where the child feels empowered to take on challenges.

Embracing the Joy of Reading

Reading should be a joyful experience, not a source of stress or frustration. For children with dyslexia, it can be easy to lose sight of this joy when reading feels difficult or overwhelming. As you implement the strategies in this book, always keep in mind that one of your primary goals is to help children rediscover the pleasure of reading.

One way to do this is by incorporating books and stories that align with the child's interests. Whether they love animals, adventure, or fairy tales, finding books that capture their imagination will make the reading process feel less like a task and more like an enjoyable activity. Read aloud to children as often as possible, and encourage them to participate by predicting what happens next, pointing out pictures, or joining in on repetitive phrases. These interactive reading experiences help children associate books with positive emotions and shared moments of connection.

Additionally, remember that reading doesn't always have to be about sitting down with a book. There are many ways to engage children with language that go beyond traditional reading. Storytelling, word games, rhyming songs, and even simple conversations about the world around them all contribute to literacy development. When children see that language is all around them and can be fun to play with, they become more open to exploring reading in their own time and at their own pace.

The Role of Collaboration

Another key theme in this book is the importance of collaboration. Teaching a child with dyslexia to read is not something that happens in isolation. It involves the combined efforts of parents, teachers, caregivers, and, in many cases, specialists like speech-language pathologists or reading interventionists. Working together as a team ensures that the child receives consistent support in all areas of their life, whether at home, in the classroom, or during therapy sessions.

As a parent or caregiver, don't hesitate to seek out additional support when needed. If your child is receiving help from a specialist, stay in close communication with them to ensure that the strategies being used are aligned and reinforced at home. Teachers, too, should be part of this collaborative effort, ensuring that the child's needs are being met in the classroom with accommodations or tailored instruction when necessary.

By working together, you create a network of support around the child, which not only helps them in their academic progress but also reinforces the message that they are not alone in their learning journey.

Looking to the Future

As you come to the end of this book, it's important to remember that teaching a child with dyslexia to read is a long-term process. While early intervention can make a significant difference, literacy development is an ongoing journey that continues well into the school years. There will be challenges along the way, but with patience, persistence, and the right strategies, your child can grow into a confident and capable reader.

This book has provided you with the foundational tools and strategies needed to get started. As your child grows and their literacy skills develop, continue to adapt and refine your approach based on their evolving needs. Stay informed about the latest research on dyslexia and reading instruction, and remain open to trying new methods or technologies that may benefit your child.

Above all, remember that your child's reading journey is unique. Celebrate their progress, no matter how small, and continue to provide them with the support, encouragement, and love they need to thrive.

8

Additional Resources

Supporting a child with dyslexia requires not only effective teaching strategies but also access to additional resources that can enhance learning. In this chapter, we'll provide suggestions for books, apps, and networks that can support parents, educators, and children with dyslexia.

Books to Read Aloud

Reading aloud to children is one of the best ways to foster a love for books and introduce them to the rhythm and joy of language. Here are some dyslexia-friendly books that can be engaging for young readers:

- **"Brown Bear, Brown Bear, What Do You See?" by Bill Martin Jr.:** This book features repetitive, rhythmic text and colorful illustrations, making it enjoyable for young children and accessible for dyslexic learners.
- **"Chicka Chicka Boom Boom" by Bill Martin Jr. and John Archambault:** This alphabet book has a catchy rhyme and engaging

illustrations, helping children learn letters while enjoying the story.
- **"We're All Wonders" by R.J. Palacio**: This picture book celebrates kindness and self-acceptance, offering a positive message for children who may feel different because of their learning challenges.

Apps and Tools for Pre-Readers

There are several apps and tools available that can support children with dyslexia in developing early reading skills, such as phonics, letter recognition, and auditory processing. These apps often use multi-sensory methods to make learning more accessible.

- **Starfall ABCs**: This interactive app teaches children the alphabet and basic phonics using a multi-sensory approach. It's engaging and fun, making it a good option for early learners.
- **LetterSchool**: This app helps children practice writing letters by tracing them on the screen, while also reinforcing letter-sound relationships. It's great for developing both fine motor skills and phonics knowledge.
- **Phonics Hero**: Phonics Hero is a comprehensive app that teaches children phonics skills through a series of games and activities. It's designed to be both educational and fun, making it a great tool for children with dyslexia.

Parent and Educator Support Networks

Navigating dyslexia can feel overwhelming, but there are numerous support networks available for parents and educators. These communities offer valuable resources, advice, and connections with other families or professionals who are also supporting children with dyslexia.

- **International Dyslexia Association (IDA)**: The IDA offers a wealth of resources for parents, educators, and professionals. Their website includes information about dyslexia, strategies for teaching children with dyslexia, and access to local chapters for support.
- **Understood.org**: This organization provides resources for parents of children with learning differences, including dyslexia. Their website features articles, videos, and tools to help parents support their child's learning at home and school.
- **Decoding Dyslexia**: Decoding Dyslexia is a grassroots movement that advocates for children with dyslexia. They offer resources for parents and provide opportunities to connect with others who are working to raise awareness and improve education for children with dyslexia.

Conclusion

Teaching children with dyslexia to read is a journey that requires patience, creativity, and a deep understanding of their unique learning needs. By using multi-sensory teaching methods, breaking down reading tasks into manageable steps, and fostering a love for books, we can help children with dyslexia develop strong reading skills and build confidence in their abilities.

This book has provided practical strategies, engaging activities, and valuable resources to help parents, educators, and caregivers support young children with dyslexia as they begin their reading journey. With the right support, children with dyslexia can become confident, successful readers who love to learn.